GW01319443

CGP

Addition & Subtraction Activity Book

for ages 6-7

This CGP book is bursting with fun activities to build up children's skills and confidence.

It's ideal for extra practice to reinforce their learning in primary school. Enjoy!

Published by CGP

Editors:
Michael Bushell, Ruth Greenhalgh and Rosa Roberts

Proofreaders:
Gail Renaud and Glenn Rogers

With thanks to Lottie Edwards for the copyright research.

ISBN: 978 1 78908 621 8

Graphics used on the cover and throughout the book © www.edu-clips.com
Cover design concept by emc design ltd.

Printed by Elanders Ltd, Newcastle upon Tyne.

Contents

Using Counting

How It Works

You can **add** to get a bigger number:

2 + 3 = 5

You can **subtract** to get a smaller number:

4 − 1 = 3

When you **add** numbers, you can **swap** them round and get the **same answer**... →

For example: 2 + 3 = 5

3 + 2 = 5

... but you **can't** do this when you **subtract**.

Now Try These

1. Count the birds and add them together.

4 + ... = ...

.... + 3 = ...

2. Cross out the right number of birds and count how many are left.

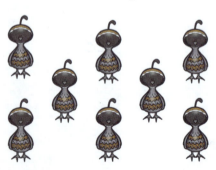

8 − 3 = ...

.... − 2 = ...

3. Below are some flamingos in a park. 7 of these flamingos are moved to a different park. Circle the number of flamingos that are left.

4. a) Danielle saw 12 birds on a branch. Then 4 more arrived.
      How many are there now?

.... + ... = ... birds

   b) 9 birds then flew away. How many are left?

.... − .... = ... birds

An Extra Challenge

Raheem spots 5 ducks, 2 woodpeckers and 9 pelicans in his garden.

3 of the pelicans move to the garden next door.
How many birds are left in Raheem's garden in total?

Write down your final calculation.

.... + ... + ... = ... birds

Are you happy using counting to add and subtract? Tick a box.

Using a Number Line

How It Works

You can use a number line to help you add and subtract.

What is **4 + 2**? Start at **4** and count **2** steps to the right:

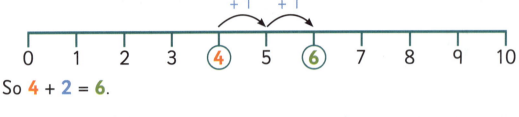

So **4** + **2** = **6**.

What is **7 − 4**? Start at **7** and count **4** steps to the left:

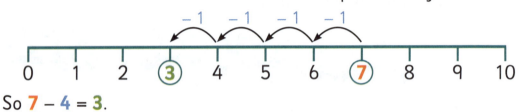

So **7** − **4** = **3**.

Now Try These

Use this number line to help work out the problems below.

1. Write the answer to each addition on the shield below the sword.

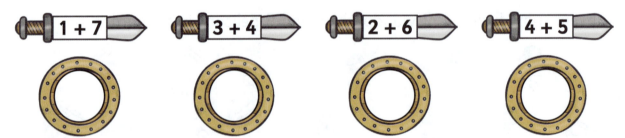

2. Work out:

7 − 1 = ☐   6 − 5 = ☐   8 − 4 = ☐

5 − 3 = ☐   9 − 5 = ☐   10 − 7 = ☐

3. Use this number line to work out the calculations below.

10   11   12   13   14   15   16   17   18   19   20

15 + 3 = ☐   17 − 2 = ☐   11 + 5 = ☐

4. Hilda has 19 coins and Erik has 4 coins. Hilda gives 8 coins to Erik.
   How many coins does each person have now?

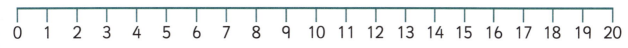

0 1 2 3 4 5 6 7 8 9 10 11 12 13 14 15 16 17 18 19 20

Hilda: .... coins   Erik: .... coins

5. The answer to the calculation below each village shows you what's sold there.
   Draw lines to match each village to the item it sells.

13 + 2   16 − 8   5 + 7

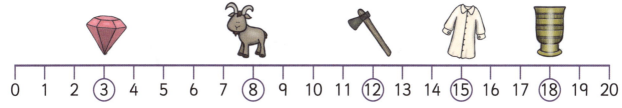

0 1 2 ③ 4 5 6 7 ⑧ 9 10 11 ⑫ 13 14 ⑮ 16 17 ⑱ 19 20

An Extra Challenge

The stones on the number line show symbols that stand for numbers.

0   1   2   3   4   5   6   7   8   9   10

Work out these calculations,
giving your answers as symbols.

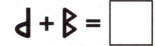 = ☐    = ☐

Number Facts up to 20

How It Works

Some number facts tell you other number facts — here's an example.

If you know this **adding** fact: $4 + 12 = 16$

Then you also know these two **subtraction** facts:

$16 - 4 = 12$ $16 - 12 = 4$

Now Try These

1. Draw lines to match knives and forks that add up to 10.

 8  10  6  4  1

 0  3  2  7  9

2. Use the number facts on the menu to answer these calculations.

$8 - 5 = $

Menu
$5 + 3 = 8$
$7 - 5 = 2$
$4 + 3 = 7$

$8 - 3 = $

$2 + 5 = $

$7 - 4 = $

3. Fill in the boxes so the sandwiches add up to 20.

 6 + 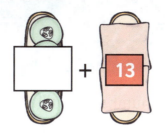 ☐ + 13  5 + ☐

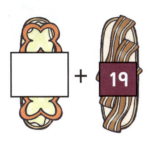 ☐ + 19  11 + ☐  ☐ + 8

4. Circle the calculation in each box that doesn't match the other two.

13 + 5	12 + 4	20 − 5
11 + 7	18 − 3	14 + 2
19 − 2	13 + 2	19 − 4

An Extra Challenge

How many ways can you combine the foods so that they add up to 20?

 19  1  9  4

  10 16  7

Tick a box to say how hungry you are... I mean, how you did.

7

Partitioning

How It Works

You can **partition** (split up) a number — it'll come in handy for adding or subtracting bigger numbers over the next few pages.

Here's how to partition **35** into tens and ones.

Look at the **place value** of each digit. $\longrightarrow$ There's a '**3**' in the **tens** place.

There's a '**5**' in the **ones** place.

So **35** is split up into **30** + **5**.

Now Try These

1. Draw a line from each number to the matching number of tens or ones.

 17

 54

 81

 48

 8 tens

 7 ones

 4 ones

 4 tens

2. Partition the numbers below into tens and ones.

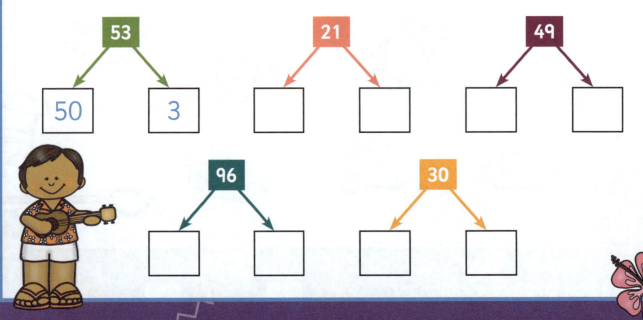

53 → 50   3

21 →

49 →

96 →

30 →

3. Write the missing numbers.

$20 + 6 = \boxed{}$

$\boxed{} + 9 = 79$

$\boxed{} + 0 = 40$

$30 + \boxed{} = 32$

4. The scores for three surfers in a competition are shown below.
   Circle the surfer who has the highest total score.

Score:
10 7 10

Score:
6 3 10

Score:
8 20 10

5. Madhuri says:

   "I am thinking of a 2-digit number. The first digit is 2 tens plus 5 tens.
   The second digit is 3 ones less than 9."

   What number is Madhuri thinking of?

   ....

An Extra Challenge

Partition these numbers into tens and ones.
What is the largest number you can make by combining the tens from one
number with the ones from another? How about the smallest number?

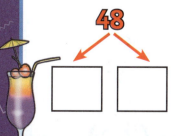

48 → $\boxed{}$ $\boxed{}$

67 → $\boxed{}$ $\boxed{}$

53 → $\boxed{}$ $\boxed{}$

74 → $\boxed{}$ $\boxed{}$

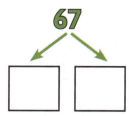
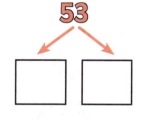
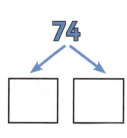

Was partitioning easy breezy?
Or does it need more work?

 $\boxed{}$ $\boxed{}$ $\boxed{}$

How It Works

You can use **partitioning** and **number facts** to make adding on and subtracting ones easier. Here's an example:

What is **53 + 4**?   Partition 53 into tens and ones.   ➝   53 = 50 + 3
                       Use number facts to add the ones.   ➝   3 + 4 = 7
                       Then put the parts back together.   ➝   50 + 7 = **57**

You can also use **number facts** to help you jump along the **number line**.

What is **63 – 5**?   63 = 60 + 3 and 5 = 3 + 2. So jumping back 3 gets you to 60, then 2 more gets you to the answer.

55 56 57 (58) 59 (60) 61 62 (63) 64 65

So 63 – 5 = **58**.

Now Try These

1. Use partitioning to work out:

   a) 31 + 7

   b) 29 – 6

   c) 67 – 3

   d) 48 + 5

2. What is 58 – 7? Colour in the party hat above the correct answer.

| 50 | 51 | 52 | 53 |

3. Draw lines to match each child with a bouncy castle.
   Each line must pass over a number in the middle to make a correct sum.

4. Use the number lines to work out these subtractions.

   a) 35 – 7 = ...

   26 27 28 29 30 31 32 33 34 35 36

   b) 41 – 6 = ...

   33 34 35 36 37 38 39 40 41 42 43

   c) 53 – 8 = ...

   44 45 46 47 48 49 50 51 52 53 54

An Extra Challenge

Tilly and Tom are jumping on a bouncy castle with some soft toys.
The picture below shows all the soft toys that fall off as they are jumping.

There were 24 soft toys on the bouncy castle to begin with.
How many are left on the bouncy castle?

How was this one for you?
Tick a box to show how you feel.

11

Adding and Subtracting Tens

How It Works

You can also use **partitioning** to add on and subtract tens. Here's how:

What is **27 + 40**?

Partition 27 into tens and ones. ➡ 27 = 20 + 7

Use number facts to add the tens together. ➡ 2 + 4 = 6, so 20 + 40 = 60

Put the parts back together. ➡ 27 + 40 = 60 + 7 = **67**

Now Try These

1. For each problem, circle the correct answer.

   a) What is 40 − 10?   30   20   50

   b) What is 20 + 70?   50   90   60

   c) What is 50 − 30?   40   80   20

   d) What is 80 − 40?   60   40   30

2. Draw lines to match each piece of seaweed to the fish with the answer.

45   28   63   15   59

 55 − 10   43 + 20   9 + 50   68 − 40   35 − 20

3. Berta asks three shrimp to solve her problem.

Colour in the shrimp that solves the problem correctly.

4. a) Sebastian has 54 shells. He gives 30 shells to his friend Bill.
   How many shells does Sebastian have left?

   ....

   b) Bill had 17 shells before Sebastian gave him 30.
   How many shells does he have now?

   ....

An Extra Challenge

Some tropical fish in an aquarium are moving between tanks.

- **20 fish** in **Tank A** are moving to **Tank B**.
- **50 fish** in **Tank C** are moving to **Tank A**.

How many fish are in each tank after the moves?

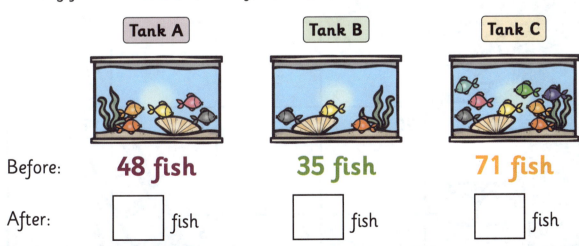

	Tank A	Tank B	Tank C
Before:	48 fish	35 fish	71 fish
After:	☐ fish	☐ fish	☐ fish

You've fin-ished these pages!
How did it go?

Snakes and Ladders

Nancy and Rhod play a game of Snakes and Ladders.
They take it in turns to roll **two dice** and move around the board, going up any ladders and down any snakes that they land on.

Follow the steps and act out the game on the board. As you go along, keep track of each player by marking the square they're on with an 'N' or 'R', or you could find two small objects to use as counters. Then, answer the question in the final step.

1   Nancy rolls a 3 and a 5. She adds them up and moves by that many places.

2   Rhod rolls a 2 and a 1. He adds them up and moves by that many places. What happens? How many extra places did he move?

3 Nancy rolls a 2 and a 4. She adds them up and moves. What happens? How many places back from where she started has she ended up?

4 Rhod rolls two 6s, adds them up and moves by that many places. How many places is he ahead of Nancy now?

5 Nancy rolls a 1 and a 5. She moves by that many places. What happens?

6 Rhod rolls the dice. The sum of the two numbers is 3 more than the total from Nancy's last roll. What number does he land on?

7 Nancy rolls the dice and lands on 'Finish'. What numbers did the two dice show?

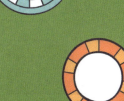

Adding Two 2-Digit Numbers

How It Works

Partitioning makes adding easier to do in your head. Here's an example. What is **27 + 32**?

Split both numbers into tens and ones: 27 = 20 + 7   32 = 30 + 2

Add the tens and ones separately: 20 + 30 = 50   7 + 2 = 9

Put the parts back together to finish the sum: 27 + 32 = 50 + 9 = 59

Now Try These

1. Work out:

   a) 16 + 52

   b) 35 + 41

   ....

   ....

2. Draw lines to match the sums on the beehives with the answers on the flowers.

| 33 + 43 | 46 + 21 | 43 + 46 | 26 + 73 |

67

76

99

89

3. Use partitioning to add these numbers.

a) 17 + 23

b) 32 + 19

4. The bee keepers are showing how many beehives they own.
Circle the bee keeper who has more beehives.

17 + 16

15 + 19

5. Amy has 25 jars of honey and Bilal has 67 jars of honey.
How many jars of honey do they have altogether?

.... jars

Queen Beatrice is thinking about her favourite number.
Which two numbers on the right add up to make it?

74

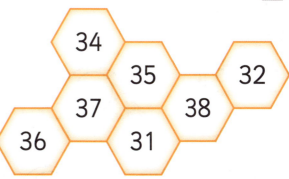

34

35

32

37

38

36

31

Do you bee-lieve in your
adding skills? Tick a box.

Subtracting Two 2-Digit Numbers

How It Works

Subtraction can be tricky, but partitioning makes it easier. Here's how you can do it. What is **67 – 25**?

Split the second number into tens and ones. ➝ **25 = 20 + 5**

Now take away the ones. ➝ **67 – 5 = 62**

Then take away the tens. ➝ **62 – 20 = 42**

You could also subtract the tens first, and then the ones.

Now Try These

1. Work out:

   a) 67 – 35

   b) 85 – 41

   ....

   ....

   c) 98 – 43

   d) 76 – 56

   ....

   ....

2. Draw lines to match each goat to its hay pile in the middle.

26 – 15

21

14

65 – 44

46 – 32

11

24

47 – 23

18

3. Use partitioning to work out these subtractions.

   a) 41 – 12

   ☐

   b) 62 – 45

   ☐

---

   c) 54 – 36

   ☐

   d) 73 – 58

   ☐

4. Zara has 97 sheep. She shears 22 of them.
   How many sheep does she have left to shear?

.... sheep

5. Dave had 85 eggs, but he lost 49 of them.
   How many eggs does he have left?

.... eggs

An Extra Challenge

Help Benny herd the sheep! Pair up the sheep so that the difference between the two numbers in each pair is always the same.

45   12   47   11   46   10

How did you find these pages?
Tick a box.

 ☐   ☐   ☐

Adding Three Numbers

How It Works

When you're adding three numbers, break it into two steps like this:

What is **3** + **5** + **7**?   Add the first two numbers: **3** + **5** = 8

Then add on the third: 8 + **7** = **15**

You get the same answer both ways.

Sometimes it's easier to add the numbers in a different order.

Look for a way to make ten: **3** + **7** = 10

Now finish the sum: 10 + **5** = **15**

Now Try These

1. Work these out in your head.

   a) 1 + 2 + 4 = ...

   b) 2 + 3 + 2 = ...

   c) 3 + 1 + 5 = ...

   d) 4 + 4 + 2 = ...

2. Haley, Chan and Jo are playing a card game — the highest score wins.
   Add the numbers to find their scores. Then circle the winning hand.

   Haley's cards:

   Score: ....

   Chan's cards:

   Score: ....

   Jo's cards:

   Score: ....

3. Tick the correct answer next to each calculation.

   a) 3 + 5 + 8   14 ☐   15 ☐   16 ☐

   b) 6 + 7 + 5   17 ☐   18 ☐   19 ☐

4. Circle all the sums that have the answer '17'.

$1 + 7 + 9$ $5 + 3 + 7$ $5 + 6 + 6$

$6 + 4 + 6$ $8 + 7 + 2$

5. The children below use their spinners to pick three numbers. They add together the numbers they pick.

a) What is the biggest number they can make?

    4 + 6 + ... = ...

b) What is the smallest number they can make?

    3 + ... + ... = ...

6. Solomon buys a board game. It comes with the following pieces: 5 counters, 8 dice and 9 tokens. How many pieces is this altogether?

.... pieces.

An Extra Challenge

Put the four tiles in the correct place on the **grid**. You must follow the **golden rule** below.

 2   5   6   9

3	8	4
7	?	?
?	1	?

Golden rule: Any three numbers in a line (going across or down) must add up to the same **number**!

Hint: use the grid to calculate the unknown **number** first.

Are you a good number adder? Pop a tick in a box!

 ☐   ☐   ☐

21

Checking Calculations

How It Works

Adding and **subtracting** are opposite calculations.
You can use one to **check** the other. Here's an example.

To check this addition...   ...do the opposite subtraction.

$12 + 15 = 27$ $27 - 15 = 12$ ←

You should get back the number you started with.

It works the other way too — you can use addition to check subtraction.

You can also check addition by adding in a **different order**.
For example, $6 + 9 + 4$ is the same as $4 + 6 + 9$.

You **cannot** check subtraction this way!

Now Try These

1. Draw lines to put everyone to bed by matching opposite calculations.

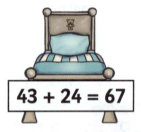

$43 + 24 = 67$

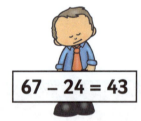

$67 - 24 = 43$

$23 + 47 = 70$

$42 + 37 = 79$

$24 + 39 = 63$

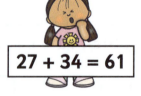

$27 + 34 = 61$

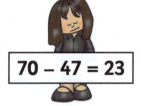

$70 - 47 = 23$

$61 - 34 = 27$

$79 - 37 = 42$

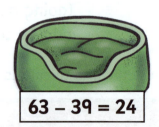

$63 - 39 = 24$

2. Fill in the boxes to complete the opposite calculations.

Calculation	Opposite

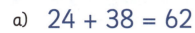

a) **24 + 38 = 62** | 62 | – | | = | |

b) **74 – 56 = 18** | 18 | | | = | |

3. Circle the addition that could be done to check each calculation.

a) 3 + 4 + 2 = 9

2 + 4 + 9   4 + 3 + 3

2 + 2 + 4   4 + 3 + 2

b) 8 + 9 + 7 = 24

7 + 8 + 8   7 + 9 + 9

9 + 7 + 8   8 + 9 + 6

4. Write an opposite calculation to check each calculation.
   Put a tick (✔) if the given calculation is right, or a cross (✗) if it's wrong.

a) 15 + 14 = 28?   .... – .... = ...   ☐

b) 48 – 37 = 11?   .... + ... = ...   ☐

An Extra Challenge

Mary counts sheep to help her fall asleep.

> I counted 26 sheep on Monday, and 35 sheep on Tuesday.
>
> That's 61 sheep altogether!

a) What calculation has Mary done?

b) What calculation could she do to check her answer?

c) Can you think of another way to check?

How did y-hraa aarh-ou do?
Tick a box!

  ☐   ☐   ☐

Missing Number Problems

Where did they go?

How It Works

Use **opposite calculations** to solve missing number problems — here's how.

What **number** goes in the box? → ☐ + 5 = 13

Write the opposite calculation. → 13 − 5 = ☐ ← Treat the box just like a number.

Then work it out. → 13 − 5 = **8**

Check you've found the right number by putting it into the box: **8** + 5 = 13 ✔

You could also answer this by thinking, "What number do I need to add to 5 to get 13?". If you know the number fact 8 + 5 = 13, then you know the answer!

Now Try These

1. Fill in the boxes with the missing numbers.

a) ☐ + 7 = 12

b) ☐ + 9 = 15

c) ☐ − 8 = 11

d) ☐ − 4 = 14

CRIME SCENE DO NOT CROSS

ruff-ruff!

2. The arrows show which thief stole the number from each calculation. Write the missing number under each thief to show who took what.

10 + ? = 13

3 + ? = 19

7 + ? = 19

5 + ? = 16

3. Solve these missing number problems.

a) 4 + ☐ = 15

b) 13 − ☐ = 6

We've got him now!

4. Detective Dan needs your help to solve his case.
   Work out the number that each shape stands for.

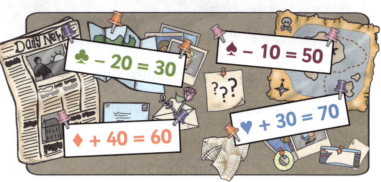

♣ – 20 = 30

♠ – 10 = 50

♦ + 40 = 60

♥ + 30 = 70

♣ = ...   ♠ = ...   ♦ = ...   ♥ = ...

5. Write the missing number in each calculation.

23 + ⬜ = 27

⬜ – 5 = 43

39 – ⬜ = 31

An Extra Challenge

Police Officer Padma has forgotten the code that locks the jail door.
Solve these missing number problems to work out the digits.

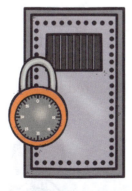

a) 3 + 4 + ⬜ = 10

b) ⬜ + 5 + 3 = 14

c) 7 + ⬜ + 8 = 20

Super-bear catches thief!

There's one more empty box
to fill — you know what to do!

 ⬜   ⬜   ⬜

25

Real-Life Problems

Now Try These

1. Draw lines to match tools so that each pair costs £35 in total.

£30   **£5**

   **£10**

£15

£25   **£20**

2. The amount of water in two buckets is shown here: Nadeem pours 16 litres of water from the red bucket into the green bucket.

22 l   **17 l**

red bucket   green bucket

a) How much water is left in the red bucket?

.... l

b) How much water is now in the green bucket?

.... l

3. Laura has measured some things in her workshop.

a) How much longer is the spanner than the pencil?

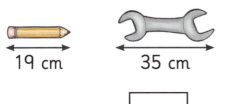

19 cm   35 cm

☐ cm

b) How much taller is the stool than the crate?

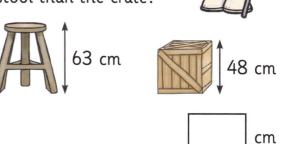

63 cm   48 cm

☐ cm

4. Jeff's wheelbarrow weighs 24 kg. He fills it with 39 kg of soil.

a) How much do they weigh together?

.... kg

b) Jeff takes 17 kg of soil out of the wheelbarrow.
   How much soil is left in the wheelbarrow?

.... kg

An Extra Challenge

Anika is selling these items at a jumble sale.

a) How many pairs of items **cost less** than £20 in total?

b) How many sets of three items **weigh more** than 20 kg in total?

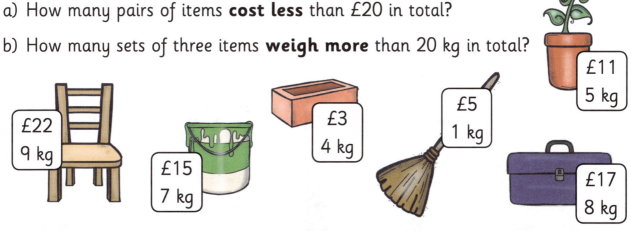

£11
5 kg

£22
9 kg

£15
7 kg

£3
4 kg

£5
1 kg

£17
8 kg

Did all your hard work
pay off? Tick a box.

 ☐   ☐   ☐

Answers

Pages 2-3 — Using Counting

1. $4 + 2 = 6$ $5 + 3 = 8$
2. $8 - 3 = 5$ $6 - 2 = 4$
3. There are $9 - 7 = 2$ flamingos left.
4. a) $12 + 4 = 16$ birds   b) $16 - 9 = 7$ birds

An Extra Challenge

There are $9 - 3 = 6$ pelicans left.
So there are $5 + 2 + 6 = 13$ birds in total.

Pages 4-5 — Using a Number Line

1. $1 + 7 = 8$ $3 + 4 = 7$ $2 + 6 = 8$ $4 + 5 = 9$
2. $7 - 1 = 6$ $6 - 5 = 1$ $8 - 4 = 4$
   $5 - 3 = 2$ $9 - 5 = 4$ $10 - 7 = 3$
3. $15 + 3 = 18$ $17 - 2 = 15$ $11 + 5 = 16$
4. Hilda: $19 - 8 = 11$ coins, Erik: $4 + 8 = 12$ coins
5. $13 + 2 = 15$ (👕) $16 - 8 = 8$ (🐘) $5 + 7 = 12$ (🪓)

An Extra Challenge

ᚦ + ᛒ = ᛮ   ᛒ − ᛉ = ᚦ
$2 + 7 = 9$ $7 - 5 = 2$

Pages 6-7 — Number Facts up to 20

1.
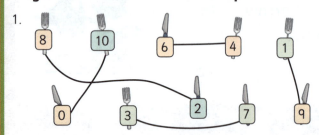

2. $8 - 5 = 3$ $8 - 3 = 5$
   $2 + 5 = 7$ $7 - 4 = 3$
3. $6 + 14$ $7 + 13$ $5 + 15$
   $1 + 19$ $11 + 9$ $12 + 8$
4.
$13 + 5 = 18$	$\boxed{12 + 4} = 16$	$20 - 5 = 15$
$11 + 7 = 18$	$18 - 3 = 15$	$\boxed{14 + 2} = 16$
$\boxed{19 - 2} = 17$	$13 + 2 = 15$	$19 - 4 = 15$

An Extra Challenge

There are four ways:

Pages 8-9 — Partitioning

1.
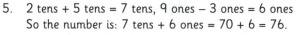

2.   53   21   49   96   30
   50   3   20   1   40   9   90   6   30   0
3. $20 + 6 = 26$ $70 + 9 = 79$
   $40 + 0 = 40$ $30 + 2 = 32$
4. 10, 7, 10: $10 + 10 = 20$, $20 + 7 = 27$
   6, 3, 10: $6 + 3 = 9$, $10 + 9 = 19$
   8, 20, 10: $20 + 10 = 30$, $30 + 8 = 38$
   So 38 is the highest total score.
5. 2 tens + 5 tens = 7 tens, 9 ones − 3 ones = 6 ones
   So the number is: 7 tens + 6 ones = $70 + 6 = 76$.

An Extra Challenge

  48   67   53   74
40   8   60   7   50   3   70   4

The largest number that can be made is $70 + 8 = 78$.
The smallest number is $40 + 3 = 43$.

Pages 10-11 — Adding and Subtracting Ones

1. a) $31 = 30 + 1$, $1 + 7 = 8$
        So $31 + 7 = 30 + 8 = 38$
   b) $29 = 20 + 9$, $9 - 6 = 3$
        So $29 - 6 = 20 + 3 = 23$
   c) $67 = 60 + 7$, $7 - 3 = 4$
        So $67 - 3 = 60 + 4 = 64$
   d) $48 = 40 + 8$
        $8 + 5 = 13 = 10 + 3$
        So $48 + 5 = 40 + 10 + 3$
               $= 50 + 3 = 53$
2. $58 = 50 + 8$, $8 - 7 = 1$
   So $58 - 7 = 50 + 1 = 51$
3. $11 + 8 = 19$ $35 + 7 = 42$
   $44 + 4 = 48$ $62 + 9 = 71$
4. a) $35 - 7 = 28$ b) $41 - 6 = 35$
   c) $53 - 8 = 45$

An Extra Challenge

9 soft toys fell off the bouncy castle. So there are $24 - 9 = 15$ soft toys left on the bouncy castle.

Answers

Pages 12-13 — Adding and Subtracting Tens

1. a) 4 – 1 = 3, so 40 – 10 = 30
   b) 2 + 7 = 9, so 20 + 70 = 90
   c) 5 – 3 = 2, so 50 – 30 = 20
   d) 8 – 4 = 4, so 80 – 40 = 40

2.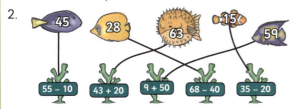

3. 74 = 70 + 4
   70 – 20 = 50
   So 74 – 20 = 50 + 4 = 54

4. a) 54 = 50 + 4
      50 – 30 = 20
      So 54 – 30 = 20 + 4 = 24
   b) 17 = 10 + 7
      10 + 30 = 40
      So 17 + 30 = 40 + 7 = 47

An Extra Challenge

1st move: Tank A loses 20 fish: 48 – 20 = 28,
           Tank B gains 20 fish: 35 + 20 = 55.
2nd move: Tank C loses 50 fish: 71 – 50 = 21,
           Tank A gains 50 fish: 28 + 50 = 78.
So after both moves, Tank A has 78 fish, Tank B has 55 fish and Tank C has 21 fish.

Pages 14-15 — Snakes and Ladders

1. 3 + 5 = 8, so Nancy moves to square 8.
2. 2 + 1 = 3, so Rhod moves to square 3.
   He then climbs the ladder to square 24.
   24 – 3 = 21, so he moved an extra 21 places.
3. Nancy moves 2 + 4 = 6 places and lands on square 8 + 6 = 14. She then slides down the snake to square 6. So she loses 8 – 6 = 2 places.
4. Rhod moves 6 + 6 = 12 places and lands on square 24 + 12 = 36. 36 – 6 = 30, so he is now 30 places ahead of Nancy.
5. Nancy moves 1 + 5 = 6 places and lands on square 6 + 6 = 12. She then climbs the ladder to square 48.
6. 6 + 3 = 9, so Rhod rolled 9. He moves 9 places and lands on square 36 + 9 = 45.
7. Nancy is 2 places away from the finish square. This means she must have rolled two 1s.

See top of next column for completed game.

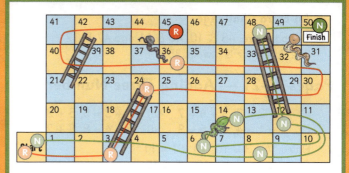

Pages 16-17 — Adding Two 2-Digit Numbers

1. a) 10 + 50 = 60, 6 + 2 = 8,
      so 16 + 52 = 60 + 8 = 68
   b) 30 + 40 = 70, 5 + 1 = 6
      so 35 + 41 = 70 + 6 = 76

2. 33 + 43 = 76 (30 + 40 = 70, 3 + 3 = 6, 70 + 6 = 76)
   46 + 21 = 67 (40 + 20 = 60, 6 + 1 = 7, 60 + 7 = 67)
   43 + 46 = 89 (40 + 40 = 80, 3 + 6 = 9, 80 + 9 = 89)
   26 + 73 = 99 (20 + 70 = 90, 6 + 3 = 9, 90 + 9 = 99)

3. a) 10 + 20 = 30, 7 + 3 = 10,
      so 17 + 23 = 30 + 10 = 40
   b) 30 + 10 = 40, 2 + 9 = 11,
      so 32 + 19 = 40 + 11 = 51

4. 17 + 16: 10 + 10 = 20, 7 + 6 = 13, 20 + 13 = 33
   15 + 19: 10 + 10 = 20, 5 + 9 = 14, 20 + 14 = 34
   So 15 + 19 is bigger, and should be circled.

5. 20 + 60 = 80, 5 + 7 = 12,
   so 25 + 67 = 80 + 12 = 92 jars

An Extra Challenge

The numbers must add up to 74. For any pair of numbers, the tens always add to 30 + 30 = 60. This means the ones must add to make 14.
6 + 8 = 14 works, so 36 and 38 is the correct pair.

Pages 18-19 — Subtracting Two 2-Digit Numbers

1. a) 67 – 5 = 62, 62 – 30 = 32, so 67 – 35 = 32
   b) 85 – 1 = 84, 84 – 40 = 44, so 85 – 41 = 44
   c) 98 – 3 = 95, 95 – 40 = 55, so 98 – 43 = 55
   d) 76 – 6 = 70, 70 – 50 = 20, so 76 – 56 = 20

2. 26 – 15 = 11 (26 – 5 = 21, 21 – 10 = 11)
   65 – 44 = 21 (65 – 4 = 61, 61 – 40 = 21)
   46 – 32 = 14 (46 – 2 = 44, 44 – 30 = 14)
   47 – 23 = 24 (47 – 3 = 44, 44 – 20 = 24)

3. a) 41 – 2 = 39, 39 – 10 = 29, so 41 – 12 = 29
   b) 62 – 5 = 57, 57 – 40 = 17, so 62 – 45 = 17
   c) 54 – 6 = 48, 48 – 30 = 18, so 54 – 36 = 18
   d) 73 – 8 = 65, 65 – 50 = 15, so 73 – 58 = 15

4. 97 – 2 = 95, 95 – 20 = 75, so 97 – 22 = 75 sheep

5. 85 – 9 = 76, 76 – 40 = 36, so 85 – 49 = 36 eggs

Answers

An Extra Challenge
The pairs are: 45 & 10, 46 & 11 and 47 & 12
(the difference is always 35).

Pages 20-21 — Adding Three Numbers

1. a) 1 + 2 = 3, 3 + 4 = **7**   b) 2 + 3 = 5, 5 + 2 = **7**
   c) 3 + 1 = 4, 4 + 5 = **9**   d) 4 + 4 = 8, 8 + 2 = **10**
2. Haley: 7 + 3 = 10, 10 + 1 = **11**
   Chan: 4 + 6 = 10, 10 + 5 = **15**
   Jo: 8 + 2 = 10, 10 + 3 = **13**
   So Chan wins.
3. a) 3 + 5 = 8, 8 + 8 = **16**
   b) 6 + 7 = 13, 13 + 5 = **18**
4. 1 + 7 + 9 (1 + 7 = 8, 8 + 9 = 17),
   5 + 6 + 6 (5 + 6 = 11, 11 + 6 = 17),
   and 8 + 7 + 2 (8 + 7 = 15, 15 + 2 = 17)
5. a) 4 + 6 + 9 = 19 (4 + 6 = 10, 10 + 9 = 19)
   b) 3 + 1 + 7 = 11 (3 + 7 = 10, 10 + 1 = 11)
6. 5 + 8 + 9 = 13 + 9 = 22 pieces

An Extra Challenge
Add across the top to find what the numbers in every line must add to: 3 + 8 + 4 = 15.

3 + 7 = 10, so this tile must be **5** to make 15.

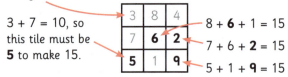

8 + **6** + 1 = 15
7 + 6 + **2** = 15
5 + 1 + **9** = 15

Pages 22-23 — Checking Calculations

1.
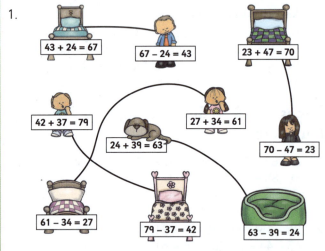

43 + 24 = 67
67 − 24 = 43
23 + 47 = 70
42 + 37 = 79
27 + 34 = 61
24 + 39 = 63
70 − 47 = 23
61 − 34 = 27
79 − 37 = 42
63 − 39 = 24

2. a) 62 − 38 = 24 or 62 − 24 = 38
   b) 18 + 56 = 74
3. a) 4 + 3 + 2   b) 9 + 7 + 8
4. a) 28 − 14 = 14 ✘ or 28 − 15 = 13 ✘
   b) 11 + 37 = 48 ✔ or 37 + 11 = 48 ✔

An Extra Challenge
a) 26 + 35 = 61
b), c) 61 − 35 = 26,   61 − 26 = 35 in either order.

Pages 24-25 — Missing Number Problems

1. a) 12 − 7 = 5, so 5 + 7 = 12
   b) 15 − 9 = 6, so 6 + 9 = 15
   c) 11 + 8 = 19, so 19 − 8 = 11
   d) 14 + 4 = 18, so 18 − 4 = 14
2.

19 − 7   12   3   16   11   16 − 5
13 − 10   19 − 3

3. a) 15 − 4 = 11, so 4 + 11 = 15
   b) 13 − 6 = 7, so 13 − 7 = 6
4. ♣ = 30 + 20 = 50   ♠ = 50 + 10 = 60
   ♦ = 60 − 40 = 20   ♥ = 70 − 30 = 40
5. 39 − 31 = 8, so 39 − 8 = 31
   27 − 23 = 4, so 23 + 4 = 27
   43 + 5 = 48, so 48 − 5 = 43

An Extra Challenge
a) 3 + 4 = 7, 10 − 7 = 3, so 3 + 4 + 3 = 10
b) 5 + 3 = 8, 14 − 8 = 6, so 6 + 5 + 3 = 14
c) 7 + 8 = 15, 20 − 15 = 5, so 7 + 5 + 8 = 20

Pages 26-27 — Real-Life Problems

1.

£30   £5   £15   £10   £20   £25

2. a) 22 − 6 = 16, 16 − 10 = 6, so 22 − 16 = 6 litres
   b) 10 + 10 = 20, 7 + 6 = 13,
      so 17 + 16 = 20 + 13 = 33 litres
3. a) 35 − 9 = 26, 26 − 10 = 16, so 35 − 19 = 16 cm
   b) 63 − 8 = 55, 55 − 40 = 15, so 63 − 48 = 15 cm
4. a) 20 + 30 = 50, 4 + 9 = 13,
      so 24 + 39 = 50 + 13 = 63 kg
   b) 39 − 7 = 32, 32 − 10 = 22, so 39 − 17 = 22 kg

An Extra Challenge
a) Four pairs:
   Paint can and brick (£15 + £3 = £18)
   Plant and brick (£11 + £3 = £14)
   Plant and broom (£11 + £5 = £16)
   Broom and brick (£5 + £3 = £8)
b) Four sets:
   Chair, toolbox, paint can (9 + 8 + 7 = 24 kg)
   Chair, toolbox, plant (9 + 8 + 5 = 22 kg)
   Chair, toolbox, brick (9 + 8 + 4 = 21 kg)
   Chair, paint can, plant (9 + 7 + 5 = 21 kg)